VENT:

Our Resilience Is Enough

A Path to Revelation, Restoration, and Reconciliation

by Mariama S. Boney, LMSW, CAE, CPEC

© MMXXI by Mariama S. Boney

Cover Image © Gloria Rosazza/123RF.COM

Printed in the United States of America

First Printing, 2021

ISBN: 978-1-953640-12-3 (paperback)
ISBN: 978-1-953640-13-0 (Kindle edition)

Page Beyond Press
Fishers, Indiana

Ordering Information:
Special discounts are available on quantity purchases by corporations, associations, and others who purchase directly from the author.
Contact mboney@achievemorellc.com for details.

Introduction

Revelation, Restoration, and Reconciliation

This devotional offers insights, and reflections for leaders to consider as we persist, persevere, and transform through the rebuilding efforts caused by political deadlock, immorality, a health pandemic, the social justice and racial equity movement, financial instability, the digital divide, and legal decay. Use the open pages to journal and share your responses to the questions. As we persist and persevere through the reality of our present times, let's get on with creating life-altering, soul-shifting change. Perhaps these times are about digging deeper and examining with greater intention our core values, beliefs, principles, truths, attitudes, and perceptions about what and who matters most in this world. All while clarifying our own culture and world view.

We must answer the call to act - respond to the call to dismantle old structures and systems. Perhaps it is about grappling with, exploring, and intentionally examining our core values, beliefs, principles, truths, attitudes, and perceptions about what and who matters most, what and who matters the least. Owning the history and telling the truth, so we can rebuild, recreate and prosper.

#Revelation #Truth #Restoration #Reconciliation

Mariana S. Boney

Educator, Executive,
Consultant, Trainer,
Coach

Table of Contents

I Am Not An Acronym

From B-I-P-O-C to L-G-B-T-Q-I-A+ to A-L-A-N-A to B-A-P, I Am Not an Acronym.

I am not a set of letters to be lumped together with others who may or may not share a common historical context, experience, or oppression.

Furthermore, I Am Not an Acronym.

I am not to be summarized by a short term that reduces my power and presence yet emphasizes someone else's privilege and status.

Therefore, I Am Not an Acronym.
I am amazing in my own right. My people, my heritage, and my culture deserve the 30 extra seconds to say – Black, African American, Hispanic, Latino, Asian, Pacific Islander, Native, Indigenous, Native American... Puerto Rican, Cuban, Iroquois, Cherokee, Kenyan, Senegalese, Chinese, Japanese... Lesbian, Gay, Bisexual, Queer, Transgender, Intersex, Asexual, or however I choose to identify!

However, I Am Not an Acronym.

See me. Value me. Include Me. Celebrate me. Let me be me.

I was born Mariama, M-A-R-I-A-M-A; Saran, S-A-R-A-N; which happens to translate in some cultures to "Beautiful Gift of G-O-D".

So, I Am Not an Acronym.

Because no gift of God should ever be reduced to a short term that reduces HIS/HER power and presence yet emphasizes someone else's privilege and status.

And take enough time to learn my name, call my name, ask M-E how I wish to I-D-E-N-T-I-F-Y.

Then, maybe, just maybe, you'll start to see that my people, my heritage, and my culture deserve the 30 extra seconds to be recognized.

Finally, I Am Not an Acronym.

I am not B-I-P-O-C or L-G-B-T-Q-I-A+ or A-L-A-N-A or B-A-P.

See me. Value me. Include Me. Celebrate me. Let me be me.
I am me — M.S.B.

In Unity,
Mariama Saran Boney
3/12/21

VENT

VENT

VENT

VENT

Week #1: Responsibility

#Much Given Much Required

"To whom much is given, much will be required…"

No longer can we ignore the systemic issues, atrocities, interpersonal wounds, cultural conflicts, suppression of dialogue, stripping of our heritage, decimation of our communities, plus eroding of the environment and our values that prevent us from moving forward as a united, collective, and collaborative force. We must remain laser focused to face this head-on, together, and act to dismantle, reframe, reshape, and innovate what we need this world to be. The future for our kids depends on it.

#revelation #truthtopower
#tellthetruth #restorativejustice
#reconciliation
#diversityequityandinclusion
#courageousleadership

Questions to Consider

- Where do you see an opportunity to shift and change?
- What truth, reality, and/or history needs to be restored?
- Who can you ask to join in the journey of creating a path forward?

"There is nothing worse than betraying yourself."

— **Oprah Winfrey**

VENT

VENT

VENT

VENT

Week #2: Listening

#Keep Listening

When you are reduced to what you think is your lowest point, I've come to understand that you must listen for what the situation, God, or the universe is trying to tell you and teach you. Sometimes the noise within us or around us is so loud, that we must step away, press pause, or re-evaluate.

Start on the journey to shift your mindset. Find ways to settle your thoughts. Remember that staying safe and healthy is a priority. Remaining emotionally solvent will enhance your self-confidence, self-worth, and self-care!

Questions to Consider

- What do you hear?
- To whom or what are you paying attention to?
- How do you focus on and act on what you are hearing?

"The mind becomes an arena where thoughts duel to the finish."

— Sarah Jakes Roberts

VENT

VENT

VENT

VENT

_____
_____
_____
_____
_____
_____
_____
_____
_____
_____
_____
_____
_____
_____
_____
_____
_____
_____
_____
_____
_____
_____

Week #3: Truth

#Face Forward

No longer can we ignore the systemic issues, interpersonal wounds, cultural conflicts, and eroding of moral priorities that move us forward as a collective and collaborative force. We must face it and move forward. Leading with a sense of hope and optimism through partnership and collaboration takes us to new heights. Defining an action plan, assigning roles, and clarifying expectations will allow you to record what works to remain relevant and celebrate achievements.

Questions to Consider

- What 2-3 situations have occurred where you need greater insight?
- Where do you need to listen more and explore further?
- How can you shift your mind to another level?

"Never forget that justice is what love looks like in public."

— Cornel West

VENT

VENT

_____

_____

_____

_____

_____

_____

_____

_____

_____

_____

_____

_____

_____

_____

_____

_____

_____

_____

_____

_____

_____

_____

_____

VENT

VENT

Week #4: Learning

#Leadership and Learning

I believe that life is a journey in learning and leadership. Everyone and everything we come into contact with presents a learning experience: A continuous opportunity to explore and discover something new as well as an opportunity to be challenged and supported to move us to a new level of understanding. It is then up to us to translate this learning into action. What are the behavioral steps that demonstrate our commitment to do something different, be better, and achieve more? At best we can utilize our individual and collective wisdom to make decisions, engage in actions, and create experiences that align with our core values, sound principles, personal strengths, and divine talents, knowing and trusting that we will find our way.

Questions to Consider

- How are you maximizing your learning?
- How does your learning impact your leadership?
- In what areas can you stretch farther?

I believe that music is good for the mind, body, and soul! Scan the code below to hear one of my favorites, if you're interested.

VENT

VENT

VENT

VENT

Week #5: Unity

#Diversity Unites

I believe that diversity is the one true thing we all have in common. When we exercise care and compassion towards ourselves and others, we can openly believe, honor, appreciate, celebrate, support, and achieve equity, access, and inclusion, plus justice for unique perspectives and experiences. Then, our level of curiosity and inquiry deepens and provides enough energy for us to stay engaged in dialogue, in relationship, and in partnership.

Questions to Consider

- How do we honor ourselves and one another?
- In what ways can we shatter the stereotypes of ourselves and others?
- When will be the time to further clarify and seek an opportunity for unity?

Scan the code below to listen.

VENT

VENT

VENT

VENT

_____

_____

_____

_____

_____

_____

_____

_____

_____

_____

_____

_____

_____

_____

_____

_____

_____

_____

_____

_____

_____

_____

Week #6: Leading through Change

#Change Leadership

I believe that people and organizations have the capacity to change and be better if they care, are committed, and have a willingness to "do the work" and do their "own work". This evolution inspires us to love what we do, care about the impact we can have, and give of our time, talents, and resources to make the world, our communities, and families healthier and happier.

Questions to Consider

- What work do you need to still do?
- What do you love to do?
- What causes do you care about the most?
- How can you give of your time and talents to be better?

" We desperately need more leaders who are committed to courageous, wholehearted leadership and who are self-aware enough to lead from their hearts, rather than unevolved leaders who lead from hurt and fear."

— Brené Brown

VENT

VENT

VENT

VENT

_____
_____
_____
_____
_____
_____
_____
_____
_____
_____
_____
_____
_____
_____
_____
_____
_____
_____
_____
_____
_____
_____

Week #7: Partnership

#Partner Up

Aligning and realigning scenarios in partnership with others for efficiency and effectiveness yield successful action plans. Thus, it is imperative that we stay connected. We can move toward success, through the challenges or trauma, and celebrate triumphs together. Allowing one another the space to be creative, vulnerable, and reflective during the process of actualizing our mission creates a pathway for innovation: an open door for who we are destined to become and the path we are defined to travel.

Questions to Consider

- Who do you need to stay connected with?
- How can you cultivate that connection for a partnership to grow?
- What is the next best step you can take to follow-up and follow-through on the connection?

"Whoever has no rule over his own spirit is like a city broken down, without walls."

— **Proverbs 25:28 (NKJV)**

VENT

VENT

_____

_____

_____

_____

_____

_____

_____

_____

_____

_____

_____

_____

_____

_____

_____

_____

_____

_____

_____

_____

_____

_____

VENT

VENT

Week #8: Exploration

#Keep Exploring

Be willing to explore what gives people hope. Explore the frustrations, the triggers, and expectations to better understand others. Consistently explore opportunities to seek out and discover something new as well as challenge and support viewpoints to move to a new level of understanding. We must admit that we don't know it all. And we can't be everything to everyone. Striving to remain authentic, be transparent, and exercise fairness is appreciated during a time when so much of the opposite threatens us each day. To stay professional, preserve respect, behave well, and practice intentionality is an opportunity for us to fine-tune the way we wish to be in the world. And when we celebrate love and remain open to giving, we will continue to grow.

Questions to Consider

- Where do you need to continue to explore?
- How can you shift to another level?
- What will allow you to stay open to new people, challenges, experiences, and learning?
- In what ways will you put yourself first to enhance your confidence and self-worth?

"At some point in life the world's beauty becomes enough. You don't need to photograph, paint, or even remember it. It is enough."

— Toni Morrison

VENT

VENT

VENT

VENT

Week #9: Connection

#StayConnected.

Always remember, you bring the very best to your brand. And who you surround yourself with makes an impact.

Find the people who provide you a safe apace and place where your truth can reside. Seek out those with whom you can share feelings, observations, fears, tears, and your perspective, in their deepest forms. And don't shy away from those who are willing to help you be better by telling you the truth, offering insights, observations, critiques, and correction. Take responsibility to nurture the connections that help you build and grow.

Questions to Consider

- With whom can you be the most authentic?
- In what ways can you take time to meet up with others?
- How will you honor time and space for yourself?

Scan the code below to listen.

VENT

_____

_____

_____

_____

_____

_____

_____

_____

_____

_____

_____

_____

_____

_____

_____

_____

_____

_____

_____

_____

_____

VENT

VENT

VENT

Week #10: Be Bold

#Bold and Brave

Be bold and brave. Don't doubt your destiny. During turbulent times we must remain steadfast and optimistic and have a mindset that anything is possible! As leaders, we have a responsibility to be hopeful. And having the foresight to create a legacy, own the risk, and innovate our way through will take us to a higher level of partnership.

Questions to Consider

- How can we flip or shift our concepts away from the traditional?
- When can we use data to set a refined course?
- What can we do to value and honor the voice within us?

"When you jump, I can assure you that your parachute will not open right away. But if you do not jump, your parachute will never open. If you're safe, you'll never soar!"

— Steve Harvey

VENT

VENT

VENT

VENT

Acknowledgements

God has blessed me! I am thankful for all the windows, doors, and blessings that have come into my life. I deeply appreciate the leadership of Bishop and Pastor Dukes at Harvest Life Church, the fellowship #HarvestLifeLeaders and my church family. I am grateful for the overflow of support in my life from my mom, sister, father, grandparents, and family in New York City, Georgia, and South Carolina; my closest sister friends from Syracuse; and my "crew", brothers and sisters in DELP, the Diversity Executive Leadership Program of ASAE. To rediscover a friendship that is healthy, honest, and kind from my love A.T. is exciting.

"Love is patient, love is kind. It does not envy, it does not boast, it is not proud. It does not dishonor others, it is not self-seeking, it is not easily angered, it keeps no record of wrongs. Love does not delight in evil but rejoices with the truth. It always protects, always trusts, always hopes, always perseveres."

— 1 Corinthians 13:4-7 (NIV)

A Path to Revelation, Restoration, and Reconciliation

Scan the codes to listen.

VENT

VENT

Be Better. Achieve More. Maximize Results.

The opportunity to impact my community, grow through courage and transparency in this world, and explore ways to be in unity and work better together are key principles that guide our work.

Achieve More LLC is a woman- and minority-owned consultancy whose mission is to help organizations and professionals be better, achieve more, and maximize results as leaders and within teams. We bring the human performance and organizational dynamics perspective, paired with an engaging, interactive, inclusive, strengths-based, and solution-focused approach to consulting, training, and coaching.

I am a certified association executive and licensed social worker in two states. I have specialized in working with associations, nonprofits, and education as an executive, trainer, facilitator, coach, DEIA consultant, presenter, and author.

Let's Connect.

https://www.achievemorellc.com/

More from Mariama S. Boney

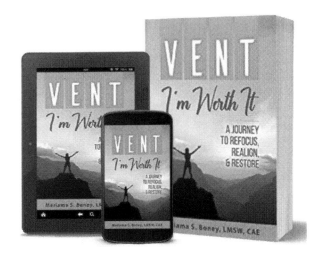

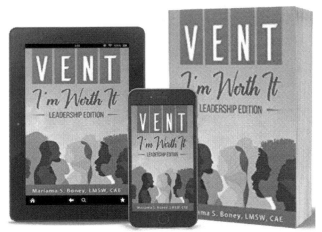

Available on Amazon

Made in the USA
Middletown, DE
23 May 2022